THE AWKWARD YEARS

Matthew Bulgo

THE AWKWARD YEARS

OBERON BOOKS
LONDON

WWW.OBERONBOOKS.COM

First published in 2018 by Oberon Books Ltd
521 Caledonian Road, London N7 9RH
Tel: +44 (0) 20 7607 3637 / Fax: +44 (0) 20 7607 3629
e-mail: info@oberonbooks.com
www.oberonbooks.com

A catalogue record for this book is available from the British Library.

PB ISBN: 9781786826695
E ISBN: 9781786826725

Cover photography: Kirsten McTernan
Cover design: Limegreentangerine

10 9 8 7 6 5 4 3 2 1

Characters

LILY – late 20s

Text in regular font is direct address

Text in italics is reported dialogue

(Text in brackets) isn't spoken and is included for clarity's sake

– indicates an interruption, either one character interrupting another or a character interrupting their own thought

… indicates the trailing off of a thought

/SHIFT/ indicates a jump in time and (sometimes) location, as if the character has closed their eyes and opened them to discover they are in a different time/place

LOCATION

The original production was set in Cardiff. The only references that locate it here are 'Womanby Street' and 'Welsh Club'. If you wish to set the play elsewhere, these two references can be easily changed.

/SHIFT/

LILY   When it comes out, it's just liquid and it burns.

Wipe my mouth and wait for the second
wave…doesn't come so I, I just sit on the
toilet and I…

Let my head slump back against the wall
and it's only then I clock my 'phone buzzing
against the porcelain.

Reach 'round, third time lucky and I –

Love?

Are you there, love?

Can you hear me?

beat, she looks around trying to work out where and when she is…

I keep her dangling there on the other end.
Or maybe it's me, maybe it's, maybe I'm the
one that's dangling.

*If you're there love you don't have to talk. Not if
you don't want to. We just wanted to know you
were okay so…*

…

<u>Are</u> you okay?

7

Mouth moves but the words get, they get
caught, they never make it to the –

*And what about work? Your dad's still not sure
you should've gone back so soon, neither am I to be
honest, I mean if it's money that's a problem, you
don't need to worry, we can cover your rent, you
just need to ask, you just need to say.*

The tiles are cold. I lift my feet onto the seat.

*We were thinking maybe we could come down and
visit? Or you could? You could come up here, we'd
like to see you, see how you are –*

I scrape the nail varnish off my toes until
there's nothing left.

*Is there anything you need, anything we can get for
you, even if it's just –*

When the words arrive, they come in fits and
starts:

*Can I – can I call you back – it's just – I can't –
I've only just woken up so –*

I never get to the other end of that sentence –

It's the afternoon, love. It's 2 o'clock.

beat

8

I stop picking at my nails and I start picking
at the paint flaking off the wall. I pick hard
and the plaster comes with it too. I pick until
there's a hole the size of my fist and I imagine
how it would feel to climb inside when it
blindsides me –

Have you been to see Jamie?

beat

*It might help if you went and talked to him, if you
just did that.*

/SHIFT/

Wake up shaking, 'phone still in my hand.

Dig my nails into my thighs and squeeze.
Watch the marks fade and go.

See the stamp on my hand, another on my
wrist, smudged, like bruises. Try and piece
the night together but it comes apart before
my mind has a chance to grip. Scrub myself
under the hot water until my hand's pink and
raw but when I dry it off they're still there, I
can still see them.

Getting back to my room is a mission, bounce
down the hallway, wall to wall, and when I
open the door it smells like someone's doused

the place in cheap whiskey. I wish I had
a match.

Take down a pint of water in one. Feel it cold
inside me. Feel it move through all my tubes.

Flop down onto the bed and something stirs.

There's a…there's a penis poking out from
under the sheets and it looks like a little, like a
little…sweaty…acorn and that makes me feel
a bit – so I – I cover it back up and I –

I try to remember his name, I'm not even
kidding – Justin, Jason – something at the
centre of my brain throbs harder and faster so
I…just stop thinking.

He sorta stirs, sorta turns in his sleep, I pull
back the covers and – from behind he could
be…but he's not…he's –

/SHIFT/

When my eyes open he's gone and I'm sort of
grateful. Hear the TV in the living room.

See the condom box on the bedside table,
see he's written his number on the little flap.
Classy.

Jackson? Jackson! Should've remembered
that.

Dry-swallow ibuprofen with one hand,
save his number with the other – *(to herself)*
Jackson?!

beat

Out of, I don't know, sheer boredom I text
him. I get as far as 'Hey'…and then I think
fuck it so I just send that.

I think about standing up. I don't. I just sit on
the edge of the bed.

'phone vibrates, text, him.

It is…*entirely* made up of emojis. A small
round face that's either sweating or crying,
three aliens, and a pair of hands that look like
their doing Nazi salutes.

I just can't help myself:

(texting) 'I'm – sorry – I – don't – speak –
moron.'

He texts straight back.

Another emoji. A small round face, laughing.

I delete his message. I delete both his
messages. Then I delete him.

beat

Check Facebook, check Twitter, check
Instagram.

I think about masturbating…but I really can't
be fucked so I check Facebook again.

I stalk school mates, uni friends, complete
strangers, scroll through photos of meals, date
nights, weddings, babies, first houses, blessed,
just saying, so lucky, fuck you, fuck you all.

When I get up the blood pumps in my ears
at a cool 200 beats per minute. I scooch up,
smoke out the window. I smoke some more. I
don't smoke.

Get the guilts, do a couple of sun salutations,
get winded pretty easy so I think fuck this for
a game of soldiers and I just lay there face-
down on the floor and feel the carpet, rough,
against my cheek –

And that –

/SHIFT/

Smell wakes me up like a brick to the face –
smoke and booze, mould and sex. Febreeze
the shit out of…everything, makes it worse –
obviously – so now I've got no choice but to
get up, to just get up and get out.

Bills on the doormat. I step over them and pad into the living room.

You look like shit. She doesn't take her eyes off the telly.

I think about saying…something. But she's right, I do, so I don't.

Kelly shifts her legs and I curl into one end of the sofa. She's texting with one hand, eating a pizza crust with the other and then totally nails a question on Roman mythology before I've even had a chance to –

See her giving me side-eyes but she's not saying anything. She knocks the telly off, walks across the room and it's all a bit vibey so I stop her in her tracks.

Well, aren't you going to ask me then?

Ask you what? She knows what.

Me and Kelly have always had this totally hilarious thing where we compare every casual shag with a film we've watched – this was when we were at uni, this was. So like when we were in halls together, and one of us brought home a random, next morning the other one would be all *so what was he like* and then one of us, whoever'd done the deed would be like...*Fast and Furious* or *Gone in 60 Seconds*...or *Deep Impact*.

she waits

Like I said, *totally* hilarious.

Once, she'd brought home this meathead, one of the rugby boys at uni, and they hadn't even done nothing yet, but as they were off to bed she turned and looked at me, square in the eye, proper dead-pan and said *There Will Be Blood* and I was gone, I was just creased.

The morning after, she's being all sheepish 'cause he's still there, hovering. Soon as he's gone I'm in, I'm like *Well then? Was there?*

And she's like *Nah...Rear Window*, dead casual, dirty cow, she was only joking but, yeah –

Anyway, pretty soon we'd done them all, the films I mean, all the funny ones anyway, so we decided to take things to a whole new level.

So...yeah, she's got up, all vibey, I've stopped her and I'm keeping her hanging, but she's not really biting so eventually I'm like:

I'm thinking maybe 2001: A Space Odyssey...

...

She's usually gagging for it but right now
she's giving me nothing, so I just carry on:

*Because, like, it was really long but not a lot
happened and then the end was just a bit confusing.*

she waits

Kelly'd laugh then. Kelly's got this killer
laugh. It's like a car back-firing. But she
doesn't. She just sorta smiles into one cheek
and this vibe, the one I was (talking about) –
it's still there so I just call her out on it:

Is there something you want to, like, say?

Still nothing but I'm like a dog with a bone
now –

*'cause it sorta feels like there is, like there is
something, so maybe you should just say it, if there
is, if there is something you want to say.*

*I was just thinking whether your boyfriend would
have found that one funny. I was just thinking
that, that's all.*

/SHIFT/

I'm at the pool. Must be Bank Holiday or
something, half term, 'cause there's kids
everywhere. No parents, just kids, and they're
all laughing, you know the way they laugh

15

so hard it's like they're screaming, the way it echoes off the walls.

And I'm scanning, scanning the pool for – when I clock I'm the only one on duty, which is, yeah, bit weird. Look from station to station and…no-one. Must've fucked off and left me to hold the fort which is, yeah, typical.

beat

Then – and-this-is-pretty-fucking-weird-but-bear-with – the kids, they all start to sink. All of them. Just start sinking to the bottom of the pool. Which is – I mean, that's just a bit nuts, isn't it?

So they say our job's prevention rather than action – scan the pool for potential problems, stop the danger at source, keep an eye on the hotspots.

But this, I mean seriously, how can anyone expect me to prevent this?

Anyway, I don't think, I just act, just like drill, just like in training. Get up and – FUCK – pain in my chest like…not like a pain-pain, more like a pressure, like a dull…like someone standing right on my fucking chest, actually.

Shrug it off – and-this-is pretty-fucking-weird-
too-but – it's hard just walking. Like, pins and
needles, like my legs, they've gone to sleep,
but worse.

Get to the edge of the pool – still-no-other-
fucker-in-sight-by-the-way – so I dive in and
that's when…

And-I-really-can't-get-my-head-around-this-
but –

I hit the water and I – I can't swim. I can't
swim a stroke. My arms are heavy, my legs
won't work, I just don't know how to –

I save one nearby, shallow end, but she
weighs a ton, struggle to pull her up, to get
her up to the surface and when I do it's…it's
me.

beat

She's got my face, which is, fuck, yeah, weird,
but no time to think, so I just move on and I –

I save another, then another, pull them up
and they're all…they're all me – they're
all – and as soon as I save them, they sink
again, and I just can't keep them all afloat, I
just can't, there's too many, and all the time
they're laughing, they're screaming and I…

I just can't do it.

I can't save them.

So I climb out, that's what I do, I climb out
and I sit in my chair and I just watch them all
sink to the bottom.

beat, she laughs shortly, then she laughs hysterically

And the *really* funny thing…is that when I
wake up, I'm sat in my chair, poolside, and
Doug's coming my way.

beat

In Doug's office there's nowhere to hide.
That's because his office isn't really an office.
It's a cupboard. In fact, it's less than that. It's
a cupboard that can't function as a cupboard
because someone's tried to put an office in it.
So in actual fact it's completely useless, a waste
of fucking space, a bit like Doug to be honest.

The first thing you need to know about Doug
is that he's my boss. The second thing you
need to know about Doug is that he's a bit of a
perve on the sly. And the only other thing you
need to know about Doug is that I've got him
wrapped around my little finger, we all have.

I sit down, all like *Hiya babe,* you know, set the tone, realise I'm still a bit pissed but fuck it, it's only Doug.

Lean back in my chair all *Come on, then. What's all this about?* I'm swigging a can of Red Bull. You know, casual.

When Doug calls you in for a 'little chat' it usually means a bit of a slap-on-the-wrist for being late or dicking around with the hose in the locker rooms or…whatever. And you nod and smile, then flirt like fuck, tell him you won't do it again and then head off to the locker rooms to dick around with the hose for a bit.

He not saying anything at first. Just sort of shifts his chair.

beat

After what feels like for-fucking-ever:

So, I know we're not due another one-on-one for a couple of months –

It's actually called a one-*to*-one but Doug always calls it a one-*on*-one because, I don't know, because I think he must get some sort of weird…sexual…'thing' out of it.

a little bullet-laugh

I imagine him having a bit of semi-on underneath the table. I imagine it pressing against the bottom of the little, kiddy desk we're sat either side of, tapping against it like an excitable…thumb. I sorta gag a bit, Red Bull comes out of my nose.

Are you okay? Is everything…?

Yeah, yeah, fine, yeah, cool, so what's up, babe?

I throw that in again – *babe* – soften him up and I'm not drinking it but I'm holding the can in front of my mouth because I just can't stop grinning now.

He reaches behind him, pulls out this folder from between all the junk and puts it down on the table.

I think I see my name written along the edge in marker pen. I twist my head to read it but the room gets a bit spinny so I just –

Well, first there's the matter of checking your phone at –

a short, sudden laugh, it's a reflex reaction

Doug. Babe. Everyone checks their 'phone at –

Yeah, well it's becoming a bit of a habit so…

And he just lets that one sit there between us.

...

O-kay.

I take a time out, take a little sip from my can.
I'm not sure how to play this so I just think
'up the ante, bring out some big guns'.

I lean in, plant my elbow on the little desk,
him inches away from me, and I start to
stroke my bottom lip from side-to-side with
my thumb, all the time fixing him with this
gaze, this gaze that could be saying *I fucking
want you, Doug* but could just as well be saying
I fucking dare you.

He breaks first – obviously – looks down, but
it's only to turn the page –

And then there's your punctuality.

I laugh. I actually laugh.

(laughing) Yeah, well –

And then there's this sleeping incident.

beat

   I –

   I wasn't –

   Sleeping?

I wasn't sleeping, Doug, I was –

I was resting my eyes so –

He's the one staring now, saying *go on, then, keep talking.*

…

And I just can't help myself, partly 'cause this is starting to seriously eat into my lunch break and partly because this hangover's turning into a real bastard-behind-the-eyes: *Doug, it's happened once, I'm tired, I was tired, I've worked three doubles this week, on the bounce, so –*

But he's not having any of it –

Yeah, well, falling asleep in a job like this, can you see how that might be a bit of a problem. I mean, technically, technically, that alone amounts to a sackable offence. You do know that, don't you. No questions asked.

He leans in, I can smell Wotsits on his breath.

I mean, there might be some jobs where you can get away with a little siesta. But a lifeguard? That doesn't really lend itself to…so it's a bit of a no-no, you can see that, can't you?

beat

Yeah, no, yeah, I can see that, no, yeah…

...

Well, if that's everything – I get up and when
I do, every piece of furniture in the room
moves, partly because I'm still a bit shit-
faced and partly because I'm in an office in a
cupboard.

That's not quite everything, no.

I can feel the heat of the lightbulb on my
forehead.

You might want to sit down.

I pick up my can. *I'm alright, thanks.* Shake it.
Empty.

*We're going to have to take some disciplinary
action, I'm afraid.*

It's all just words now and I'm not really
hearing them because…because I am fucked.

*I don't want to have to let you go. I will fight your
corner but –*

He takes out this envelope and slides it
across the table with his little cocktail sausage
fingers. He doesn't look at the envelope, he
looks at me.

That's a final warning.

beat, she's a UXB, anything could happen

> *Doug, are you fucking kidding me, I closed my eyes*
> *for, like, five minutes, <u>five</u>, nobody got hurt, nobody*
> *died, in fact, do you know what, I've worked here*
> *for ten years on-and-off, since I was in uni, ten*
> *years, and do you know how many people I've had*
> *to pull out of that pool, in ten fucking years...*
> *<u>zero</u>, that's how many, so I don't know why you're*
> *having such a shit-fit about it, a final warning, are*
> *you fucking kidding me, I just closed my eyes.*

<u>Fuck sake</u>.

Once I've got it all out, there's sweat on
the back of my neck. The room's hot and it
throbs and it presses the air out of me.

I know things must be hard right now –

Do you?

I mean, I can't even imagine –

Can't you? What, imagine what?

Well –

Something in the room makes a sound and
when I look down I see it's the can, crushed
in my hand, twisted metal.

Maybe you need to take some more time off. I'm not
blaming you, no one's blaming you and there's

24

something about that, those words, the words he says, that just –

Yeah, you know what, I think you're right, Doug.

I think I do need some time off now you've come to mention it.

I think I probably need a fuck-ton of time off, actually.

I don't think I'm going to be coming in tomorrow.

I don't think I'm going to be coming in for the rest of the week.

I don't think I'm going to be coming in ever again to be fucking straight with you.

Yeah, I reckon you can take this final warning and you can ram it right up your arse crack, probably.

Doug's not saying anything now. Which is probably for the best.

When I open the door, the cold air gets inside me, it fills me up and cools me down.

I almost get out the door when he stops me.

You – you don't mean that.

Don't I?

I am really sorry, you know.

Go on, Doug. Pull the trigger you wet-wipe. *Sorry? What have you got to be sorry about?*

Well…

Well, everything with Jamie.

/SHIFT/

Wake up on the sofa and there's blood in my mouth 'cause I've been grinding again.

Spit into the sink 'til it's clear, drink from the tap, get some toothpaste on my finger and I rub it about a bit.

I make two slices of toast and I practically swallow them whole.

Make another two and they suffer the same fate.

Another two and I actually start to feel human again, so all that's left to do is to get Kelly on side.

Kelly and Kyle are in bed watching…some shit on Netflix…and I'm like no, just no.

I sort of launch myself into the middle of them.

Kelly looks at me like whatthefuckyoudoing
but by now I'm sorta cwtched in between the
two of them.

Do you want to maybe, like, knock?

When have I ever knocked, Kel, seriously.

*Yeah, well we could've been up to anything in here
so –*

Yeah, well you weren't, were you, so –

I can feel Kyle blushing next to me, I mean
there's some serious heat coming off him.

And Kyle doesn't mind, do you Kyle? I sort of
rub his thigh, you know jokes but it's all a bit
much for him so he shuffles off to the kitchen
and I hear him flip the kettle on.

Well?

Well what? she says.

Well, you can't go out like that, can you?

Not going out, am I. She bats it straight back at
me.

I give her this look that says 'oh, I think you
are' but she's not having any of it.

Anyway, haven't you got work in the morning?

beat

I side-step that but before I get a chance to
regain my balance –

*And I thought you were skint anyway. Did you see
the bills? Because you still owe me for the last lot,
so –*

I side-step again and this time I try and
shut her down: *What we talking about bills for,
Kel?! It's Friday night for God sake! Bring Kyle.
I don't care!*

she waits a tiny beat

GOD! Don't be so fucking BORING!

beat

We're caught in some sort of weird Mexican
stand-off, neither of us wanting to make the
next move in case it's the wrong one.

She breaks first: *yeah, well, we sorta said we'd
have a cwtchy night in so –*

*CWTCHY NIGHT IN?! Fuck me! Fine! I'll go
out by myself. Find some people, latch onto some
randoms. Maybe someone'll find me dead in a gutter
tomorrow morning. Hey – maybe they'll ask you to
come and ID my body! That'll be fun, won't it!*

So don't go out. If you don't want to end up in a
gutter, don't go out.

God, Kel. You used to be fun. Remember when you
used to be fun?

beat

As far as vibes go, it's not a great one.

Kelly just sorta cuts straight through it: *don't*
you think you could do with a night off? You've
been out every night, I have noticed as it goes,
hardly seen you.

I try and come back at her but –

And since you mentioned it, don't you think you've
brought home more than enough randoms the last
coupla weeks.

I feel the blood jump to my skin but before
I get a chance to sink me teeth in she jack-
knifes me –

Have you even been to see Jamie?

beat

Because I have. I went to see him today. I talked to
him. Don't you want to know how he is?

I feel my eyes start to go, like they want to
close, so I dig my nails into my palm.

Don't you think that if I wanted to talk about him then I'd talk about him. Only I get to bring him up. Nobody else. Only I can do that –

I feel something start to shake, my guess is it's me –

Yeah, well, maybe burying your head in the sand isn't –

I LOST MY FUCKING JOB YESTERDAY, KEL – I GOT SACKED – SO DO YOU WANNA JUST –

beat

The tears come quick, the tears then the snot, then I find it hard to breathe and it sorta takes me by surprise, sorta surprises us both to be honest.

She's just sitting there with her forehead all scrunched up.

You – you shoulda said –

YEAH, WELL I DIDN'T WANT TO TALK ABOUT THAT EITHER, DID I?!

She puts her hand on my back and I…I just go, I'm lying in her lap now on the floor. She's holding me, my head resting against her belly.

I'm sorry, Kel – I'm still sorta gasping for breath *– I'm a dickhead. I don't mean to be, I just – I'll be better. I will. I just – Right now – I just need to go out. That's what I want right now.*

She puts her chin on my head, plays with my hair.

I can feel Kyle standing in the door, can feel her mouthing something but I don't know what.

Can't we –? Can't we just go out, Kel? Like we used to. I just need for us to go out. Go out, get fucked, dance like maniacs, like we used to, remember? I'll be back on form soon, I will, I promise, but now I just need that – I need you. You're my bestie, you know that.

I don't hear it but I feel it – she sighs, I feel her deflate…and that's when I know I've got her.

Give me 20 minutes. She gives me a little flick. *But I want to be home by midnight!*

When I look up at her, I can't help grinning. *I don't know what I'd do without you.*

She smiles then, smiles into one cheek…but there's something else just underneath.

/SHIFT/

The bar…is a wreck.

It just doesn't know what it wants to be, so it's tried to do it all and, pretty much, failed at everything.

It's gone Soho Chic, but with bargain basement prices. It's gone members club aesthetic but it does Ibiza-themed Thursdays. It's the kind of place that has Jaegermeister on tap. I mean – it's a fucking disaster is what it is.

And the only thing any of us can do is drink, to forget this ever happened.

beat

I fucking love it.

Get back from the bar and: *I know it was my round but Rhys – this-is-Rhys-by-the-way – he very kindly offered to buy me a drink so –*

Out of the corner of my eye I see Kyle feign a yawn and Kelly sorta shifts in her seat as if to say *well this has been lovely but we really should bounce.*

Rhys and me, we slip into the booth next to them, block their escape and it's not until we're sat down that I get a good look at him. Rhys is all bleached highlights and gap year

32

jewellery. I realise I'm not nearly drunk
enough for this.

I drain my glass in one. I dribble a bit
but I style it out, in fact I sorta turn it into
something quite sexy truth be told.

I put it down, smile, sorta shrug as if to say
wow I must've been thirsty and as if by magic
Rhys is toddling back to the bar to get me
another double…another double of…another
double of whatever that was.

Kelly says my name.

Says it again but I'm not giving her anything.

I just nod to the music, look out onto the
dance floor.

She grips my shoulder, tight:

We're going.

What?

We're going to go.

What now?

Yeah.

What? Right now?

Yeah.

Go right now?

Yes.

Really?!

I keep shoving that stick in her spokes and buy just enough time for Rhys to get back with my drink.

Well, you might as well have one more now. It's early, anyway!

It's gone one. We're going. Probably best if we share a cab, don't you think.

Rhys slides in beside me in the booth and – *bold* move – goes straight in with the arm. Over the shoulder, under my armpit and almost within reach of my side-boob and… there's something, something about that that –

When I look at him, he's got this grin like a… like a competition winner.

He's served his purpose so I throw him under the bus.

Woah there, mate. Bit handsy.

What – I – I thought – I thought we were –

(coldly) What? What did you think?

beat

*(breaking with a smile) Wait, you didn't –
(giggles) Oh, God, you didn't think I was like…
into you or anything did you? (giggles) Oh God,
no! I just saw you and I thought…I thought – can
I be honest with you, Rhys – it is Rhys, isn't it?
– No, I thought to myself 'Aww God, he looks like
he hasn't had a good fuck, well any sort of fuck in
fact, in a very long time – am I right?*

I'm having fun now so I just keep on
pumping my legs.

*No, I looked at you and I thought…all I've got to
do here is give him a grin, one that says just enough
but not too much, I've just got to catch his eye as I
drain the last dregs of drink through my straw, my
body ever-so-slightly angled towards him – all I've
got to do is that and he'll be falling over himself
to buy me a drink, he won't be able to get his cash
out quick enough, he'll order me a double, a treble,
a large, whatever I want, because he'll be thinking
that's the drink that's gonna seal the deal, that's
the drink that's gonna get me a bit of 'thunder
down under' – am I sorta warm because I think
I'm sorta warm?*

He's got these glassy, puppy-dog eyes now
that are saying:

35

Please put me down.

Please make it painless.

Please make it quick –

No, see, I've got news for you, and it's not the good sort of news, it's the kind of news that's sorta gonna really screw with your night, to be honest.

Kelly's giving me side-eyes but I can see inside she's thinking *whatthefuckwhatthefuck –*

Yeah. See. I just wanted a drink.

beat

And you bought me one – two in fact – so, yeah, nice one, thanks for that…but…what else would you do? I can feel bits of my brain start to crumble and float off up towards the ceiling. *I mean, would you run through a brick wall for me? Would you run into a burning house to pull me out? Would you, if I was like choking to death right here and now, would you know what to do? Would you?*

Because if not, if the answer to any those questions is no, then I don't think – and I'm just being honest here, Rhys – but I don't think you're the man for me. You see, I have very high expectations.

He's not saying anything, no one is, so I just keep on talking –

So, yeah, that's it. I wanted a drink. And I looked at you and I thought…he'll do that. He'll buy you a drink. So if you thought anything else, then that's…well, that's…hilarious, <u>hysterical</u> to be honest. I mean look at you. Look at the state of you. Mate.

Someone says my name –

'cause unless you're a Maori, or a pirate, or you're in a 90s boy-band, you can't really get away with that shit. All this frayed rope and beads. Shells and shit. I mean, come on, who wears flip-flops to a bar? WHO?!

Someone's tugging on my arm but I'm just –

Do you feel like a bit of a twat? Because you look like a bit of a twat. You do.

Kelly pulls me away, Kyle's shuffling after like her gormless sidekick.

I was enjoying myself then. Don't you want me to have fun?

It's like she's taken the handbrake off now 'cause she's coming at me full-throttle:

You're being a dick and if no one else is going to tell you then it's going to have to be me, and I know you have shit on your plate right now, bad shit, but right now you need to get a grip, get a grip and get on with things, instead of being like this, instead

37

of being a dick. In fact, you know what, you're not
even being a dick, you're being a real ugly cunt is
what you're being actually and I'm not going to
let you get away with it any more, I'm not letting
you get away with it because I'm your mate, and
mates are meant to look out for each other, mates
are meant to tell each other shit like that, to tell the
truth, so that's what I'm doing, I'm telling you the
truth. You're being a dick.

beat, she smiles faintly

I feel like grabbing onto something plain
nasty, and just hurling it at her...so I do –

Can I – can I just stop you there because – and it's
funny you should say all that about truth – because
there's something, and I've been dying to tell you
and now sorta feels like the right time – the perfect
time in fact – to say it. You see, I didn't get sacked.

I swear I can actually see the moment she hits
boiling point.

No, see, yeah, I made that up. Truth is I quit. I
told them to shove it, so, yeah, sorry to hijack your
'cwtchy night in' and all that –

She says something but I don't hear it – *what*
was that? – and I try, try and focus, on her
mouth, but the room it, it starts to tilt.

She says it again and this time it lands and it
breaks the skin.

I'm moving out.

beat, we don't know whether she's going to laugh, cry or explode

You –

You fucking what?

*I'm moving out, I'm moving in with Kyle, I was
gonna do it before, I was going to do it months ago,
but when everything happened with Jamie –*

And when she says that, something inside me
starts to shake.

*I can't keep picking up the pieces. I can't be around
you if you're gonna be like this. You need help, you
need to move back home and if me moving out is
the thing that makes you do that, the thing that
makes that happen then maybe that's for the best.*

And I don't choose to do it, it's not a
conscious thing – but now she's wearing
my drink, it's dripping off her chin and now
neither of us knows what's coming next.

She says it again, says his name again, and I
feel my seams start to split –

*If Jamie was here, if he could see you right now,
he'd be disgusted, in fact, no, do you know what, he*

wouldn't be disgusted, he'd be fucking heartbroken
is what.

Her lips are still moving but I can't hear the
words –

Room tilts and –

Stomach starts to –

Glass drops, shatters and –

/SHIFT/

Spew hits the ground before my foot hits the
pavement. Stand up, air hits, everything starts
to –

Walk, keep on walking, just keep on walking
up Womanby Street –

Hand out of jeans, close one eye and count, 5
quid in change and it's going on Welsh Club –

Spread on the desk, don't wait for the stamp –

Music thuds, blood pumps, something in my
gut tries to punch and I –

Top of the stairs, through the doors, band on
stage, all fringes and elbows, angles and jerks,
snarl and howl, crowd cheers, I want to stamp
and clap and dance and destroy –

We've been – and the singer shouts, and it sounds like – *(giggles)* sounds like he says 'The Awkward Years' – *you don't know the fucking half of it, mate!* Faces turn and look, stare right back, I'm spoiling for something but I don't know what –

Double vodka and coke, words drip out, try again and this time he gets it, take it and run and down it in one –

Minesweep for more, lager, cider, vodka coke, Jack and ginger, all tastes the same, stomach swells, cramps, like there's something – someone through the lights, smoke, bodies, boy on the dance floor, see a boy from behind, see a boy and it could be, could be, but it –

Both hands, grab his shirt, – *what's your name?* Says Freddie, says his name is –

You don't look like a Freddie, you don't look at all like a – you look like a Jamie, think I'm going to call you – is that cool with you? Is that cool with you if I –? Is that –

Laughs, and that smile, that smile, it could be his, but it –

Dribble, style it out, sexy in fact –

I hurt everyone I meet. I break everything I touch. I fuck up everything I put my mind to but the words, they come out all (jumbled) they all come out (jumbled), he smiles, nods, laughs 'cause he can't hear, can't hear a word I'm, 'cause the music, the music, it's, so I lean in –

Do you want to get fucked? Do you want to get really fucked? I want to get really fucked –

Says home, says something about home – *My place is miles away but we could go back to yours, so –*

Says it again –

You should go home? Maybe you should go home? Are you by yourself?

I'm with you I say, and I smile, I try and smile, and I hold on tighter.

I'm with you, and I pull at his shirt, and the night tilts even more.

Want to be fucked numb, want to consume myself, want to melt into the dance floor and get stamped on, want to soak into the wood, want to drip through the cracks.

Says he'll call a cab, says he'll pay, still holding his shirt, girl walks up to us, nearly pretty, she's nearly – *Who's this? – Who are you?* Stomach empties, floor slips under me,

foot on my hand, I don't care, eyes close and
I'm lifted, being lifted –

You're a mad one, aren't you, hear someone
saying it but my eyes won't –

Music muffled like under water and up for air
and I'm out, out on the street – and the floor's
a wall I'm leant up against.

Eyes open.

beat

Head for doorway – hand stops – *think you've
had enough – have I fuck?* – kick chips through
the door – and I walk – keep on walking –
open eyes, close and –

/SHIFT/

Leant against something and it's cold – it's
cold and it's hard – eyes want to close and –

/SHIFT/

Lads, down the street, tight shirts, pointy
shoes, *waheeeey* – and it's him – I see him –
but it's not – try and look again but I can't,
'cause my eyes won't –

/SHIFT/

'Phone in hand – voicemail – leave a message
– try and tell him but the words won't – and I
remember – try and keep on walking but my
eyes won't –

/SHIFT/

Open – table – bright light – shakes my –
name badge – can't read it – *time to go home,
love* – but it's not – still shaking my – hand on
arm – under my – kick out but my eyes won't –

/SHIFT/

Street – doorway – rain on my face – think I
taste blood – think I taste –

Close eyes, close them and –

/SHIFT/

Cab, flag it down, flag it, but it – cab won't
take me – cab won't – cab won't take me, cab
won't fucking – kick out, kick, floor slips, eyes
close and –

/SHIFT/

Rain – and the taste – taste of – closing, eyes
closing and –

/SHIFT/

Girls – one runs, turns, flashes knickers –
house party! – shout it back, but the words –
the words won't – fall in line behind, but the
rain, the rain – eyes close and –

/SHIFT/

Open – cab – backwards – wrong way 'round
– someone smiles – eyes closing but I hear
her, hear her laugh – *is she alright? – COURSE
I'M FUCKING (alright)* – never hear, never
get to the other end of –

/SHIFT/

Lifted – *I can walk – she's smashed, she's –
(laughing) don't know the fucking half of it* –
knees on ground – find wall and lift – comes
out, just liquid – hand on back, on shoulder,
on side – kick out, something kicks and I –

/SHIFT/

Stood – in the light – move, move to the
music – here it is, second wind – clothes wet
but I'm warm and that –

/SHIFT/

Stood and they're sat – room turns – faster –
see him – could be – room spins – can't find
him, can't, and I remember, I –

/SHIFT/

Glass of red – fuck it – tip it up – on my
head – down my face – *she's <u>that</u> guy!* – hear
someone say it – *I'm <u>that</u> guy* – cheers – red
– see the colour – on my hands – my clothes
and –

/SHIFT/

Pain – pain in my – pressure – drink – drink
through it – dribble – sexy – drink – eyes –
close –

/SHIFT/

Carpet, rough on my –

/SHIFT/

Red and it's –

/SHIFT/

Wet and I –

/SHIFT/

Hand on my –

/SHIFT/

Him and it's –

/SHIFT/

Him and I –

/SHIFT/

Him on my –

/SHIFT/

Him –

/SHIFT/

Him –

/SHIFT/

Him –

/SHIFT/

Him –

/SHIFT/

Him –

/SHIFT/

Him –

/SHIFT/

Him –

/SHIFT/

Eyes open…

…

Sofa's wet…

…

Wet and I check and it's me.

Eyes want to close, want to – open, keep
them, and I…

Out the door, shoes gone, doesn't matter…

The streets, the names, don't mean anything,
so I walk, middle of the road, walk the line,
towards the lights, I see them, so I walk, keep
on walking, closer, keep on walking, a little
further, and I try and shout, into the light,
move my mouth, nothing left, so I walk, just
keep on walking, into the light, into the warm
– into the traffic – into the light – into the
warm – into the light – into the traffic – into
the warm – into the light – into the warm –
into the traffic – into the –

/SHIFT/

When he picks up, I can tell he's been
sleeping. He tries to shake it off but he just
can't.

Tell him there was this party, tell him I've
tried flagging a cab, tell him I'm a bit pissed –
he knows where this is going.

It's 3 in the morning he says, and he tries
to grumble about me waking him, tries to
grumble about being on an early in the
morning, but he just can't keep it up.

Gimme twenty he says, still trying to sound
narked, and ten minutes later I can see him
rounding the corner.

And by the time he pulls into the curb, and
by the time I get in the car, and by the time
I buckle up, out of the dark his eyes are
sparkling at me…and mine are sparkling
back.

an embarrassed beat

Curl into his shoulder as he wraps his arm
around me – over my shoulder, under my
arm – and he just holds me there, tight.

Shut my eyes and I listen to him talk, he tells
me things, silly things, about his day, one arm
wrapped around me, one hand on the wheel
and he –

beat

He stops, halfway, must've closed his eyes,
that's what must've happened, 'cause he
stops, halfway through a thought, it's funny,
but by now, I can't open my eyes, by now I'm
gone and –

It's the screech, of the tyres, that makes me
open my eyes, see the car speed towards us
and he…

He turns – Jamie – to the left. Turns the car.
Everything seems to stop, and in that moment
I think –

…

And this might sound –

…

But I think he did that on purpose, I think
that's what that was, he made a choice, and
it was to save me, he'll take it all, the impact,
and if he did, if that's what he did, if he did
do that then…

beat

I think that might be –

I think that might be what love is.

If someone asked me, that's what I'd say, I
think.

And just as soon as I think that…that's when
it hits –

/SHIFT/

I walk, I must've walked, 'cause I'm in the
road now, try and suck in air but my chest,
the pressure, walk, walk through it, keep on
walking, legs won't, see a light, flag it, flag it
down, ground moves under me and –

/SHIFT/

Rain on my cheek, ground's cold and it's
hard, feel it rough on my face, walked,
must've walked, can't move, pressure in my,
mouth warm but it's just blood, I can taste it
and I –

/SHIFT/

See my 'phone on the tarmac, and I reach,
skin tears, broken glass, doesn't matter, keep
on reaching, 'cause if I can reach, if I can just
reach out, if I can just reach a little further,
then I'll call him, I'll call and I can tell him,
and he'll know, he'll know what to do, he
always does, he'll know and everything will
be –

beat

But then I remember –

/SHIFT/

Love?

Are you there, love?

Can you hear me?

I'm reaching out before I've opened my eyes
and now there's a hand holding mine.

You don't have to say anything. Stay with me, love.

The hand slips away and before the room
comes into focus, she's gone.

I roll over and sit up in one sharp move, and
the shooting pain tells me that might not have
been the best idea I've ever had.

Try and stand, something snags – tubes and
wires – I pull until they give and walk out into
the hallway.

At the door, a pair of hands meet me, turn me
'round and guide me back the way I came,
and a voice asks me questions.

Can you remember being brought here?

I feel the heat of her through the gown I'm
wearing and there's something about that that
makes my eyes water.

Can you remember what happened to you?

She says I can just nod or shake my head but
I don't do either.

*You really shouldn't be up and about in your
condition*

And right then, sat on the edge of that bed, I
can't piece it together, any of it, so it all just…

beat

You've been very lucky. Both of you.

And I think Jamie, I think she must mean
Jamie and me so I say his name, and when
I do, it's like my mouth belongs to someone
else. Say it again, and when she looks at me
I can see there's something underneath, but I
don't know what.

Mum tears into the room but when she sees
the nurse she settles.

Jamie's upstairs the nurse says

beat

He's two floors up. Right above you in fact –

Is he…?

The same she says. *He's the same –*

But both. You said both.

Their eyes meet and I think I see the nurse
shake her head.

53

Perhaps it's best if I show you she says. So that's
what she does.

/SHIFT/

At first, I can't see it. She tells me where to
look but to me it's just a mess, white splotches
on black.

She traces a line with her finger, joining dots.
She says *that…that's the head…*and once I see
it I can't see anything else.

beat

She asks if I have questions.

It's…is it –

*It's fine. It's healthy. You're going to have to start
looking after yourself though.* Mum's not saying
anything but I can feel her eyes.

*Did you have any idea? Were you even trying for
a –*

I just shake my head and keep on looking.

*16 weeks. It's 16 weeks. We can't tell the sex – not
just yet – but give it another fortnight.*

But I'm not really listening…because all I can
think is it's his – it's Jamie's.

beat

> She asks about my period. Tell her I'd missed
> it but I'd thought it was the stress, that I'd
> read that it could be that – so that's what I'd
> thought, so –
>
> *And vomiting?* I just nod 'cause suddenly I'm
> scared to move in case this tiny thing inside
> me falls apart.

beat

> She holds my hand, my mother's holding the
> other. She says we have a window, a small
> one, a bit of breathing space, but that I should
> put some thought into…whether I want to
> keep it or not
>
> She leaves us then, the nurse.

beat

> Mum drags her chair closer. She doesn't
> say anything. She doesn't have to. She just
> squeezes my hand.
>
> I can't look at her. I can't.

silence

> *When I didn't go and see him, that wasn't because
> I didn't…care.*

It's because I – I couldn't see him like that and know…that it'd been me that…

That it'd been my…

She squeezes tighter, she's hurting my fingers now, but I just let her.

No one's saying anything. I hear every click, beep, creak, hiss.

beat

Well, if you did want to see him…you know where he is.

She gathers up her bag, her coat.

Your things are in the cupboard. I can get them if you like.

I can do it.

She smiles, she tries to smile, then she goes.

beat

I empty the plastic bag into my lap. Purse. Keys. Mobile. A crack right across the screen.

Press the power button, hold it down hard, harder, nothing, dead.

There's sweat on my forehead from the effort.
I fall back into the pillow.

I close my eyes, open them. Close, open.

Still here.

beat

Out in the corridor everything's still. I twist
out of bed, pad out the door, and when I get
there...I just keep on walking.

There's a pain in my hip, another in my ribs
but I breathe through it and I keep on driving
my legs.

I take the lift – two floors up – and when the
doors slide open I step out. The pain glows
brighter, throbs harder but I just keep on
going.

beat

When I get to the doorway, I somehow know
it's him, know he's lying there in the dark, so
I step inside.

I watch the machine helping him breathe, see
it move up and down, watch his chest move
with it and my own breathing falls in sync.

beat

I lift his hand in mine.

I put it on my stomach and I hold it there,
tight.

beat

And something twitches into life. But I don't
know what.